SINGAPORE
historical
POSTCARDS

Introduction by Lily Tan, Director, The National Archives
Edited by Gretchen Liu
Designed by Viscom Design Associates
Research by Lim Guan Hock and Lisa Lim Kheng Tin

Photography by Mrs Judy Milliman, Chng Wak Hock, Ainon binte
Bahari, Peter Chen
Typesetting by Superskill Graphics Pte Ltd
Colour Separation by Sixty-Six Lithographic Pte Ltd
Printed by Tien Wah Press

© Times Editions
All postcards © The National Archives except
© Koh Seow Chuan, P7 top right; Postcard 141
© Andrew Tan Kim Guan, p.7 top left; bottom left, bottom right; p.13
    bottom; Postcards 88, 105, 106, 113, 114, 124, 147

Cover: The Chartered Bank Building on the corner of Battery Road and
Flint Street housed the bank from 1895 to 1905. Balanced, gracious and
classical in design, it stood in marked contrast to the extravagant
Hongkong and Shanghai Bank Building across the square in the left of the
postcard. The contrast between the two demonstrates the enormous
variety of architectural styles transplanted to Singapore.

Back Cover: Tanjong Pagar Road

ISBN: 9971-40-045-6

SINGAPORE
historical
POSTCARDS

From the National Archives Collection

TIMES EDITIONS

Panoramic View from Fort Canning Hill, circa 1890s.

CONTENTS

INTRODUCTION

Picture postcards have been with us for so long that we tend to take them for granted. Very few people know when or why picture postcards were invented.

The idea of an economical open means of communication had been promoted by two Europeans around the same time — but independent of each other. The Director-General of the Austrian Post, intrigued by the idea, issued the first official postcard — the *Korrespondenze Karte* — on October 1, 1869. This was less than 30 years after the "coming of age" of postal services with the introduction of the first adhesive postal stamp in England in 1840, the famous "Black Penny". Many countries followed the Austrian example and soon postcards were crossing the world at a remarkable rate.

The Straits Settlements (the three settlements of Singapore, Penang and Malacca under British Colonial Government rule) issued its first postcard in 1879. These blank postcards to which a stamp had been affixed were available only through Post Offices. For the next 15 years only "official" postcards enjoyed the special rate of three cents for international distribution from the Straits Settlements. As privately produced postcards cost the same as a full letter, few were produced and circulated. Then, in 1894, the British postal authorities amended their regulations so that private postcards could be despatched at the same inexpensive postal rate. By 1898 privately printed postcards with pictures began to appear in the market. The 1898 Straits Settlements Annual Report described picture postcards as "artistically got up with characteristic local views." And so began Singapore's picture postcard industry, capturing the memorable scenes, people and special events seen in these pages.

At first only the recipient's address could be written on the back of the card and messages were written in white space left along the bottom or the side of the picture. After 1902 messages could be written on the backside and the images expanded out to fill the entire card. The black and white images were then spiced up with colour. "Oilette" or painted scenes also gained popularity. On many post-

North Bridge Road, Singapore.

Could the two men in the postcard be postcard hunting? Kong Hing Chiong's shop at the Adelphi Hotel stocked "Picture Post Cards of Singapore, Johore and the F.M.S."

Visions of the past. Clockwise from top left: Across the Padang where City Hall and the Supreme Court now stand; barren land after Telok Ayer Bay reclamation with Cecil Street and Robinson Road laid out; a park-like Raffles Place and a bustling Battery Road circa 1900.

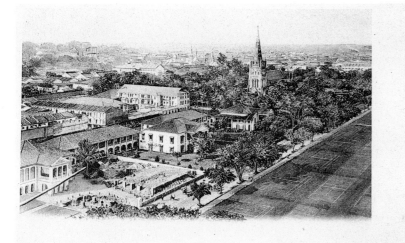

Singapore. Blick auf den Hafen.

Singapore. Battery Road.

Singapore, Raffles Square.

Kelantan 27.3.05

cards a number indicates that the card is one of a series. Picture postcards soon became collectibles, just like matchboxes for instance.

A look at the imprints on the reverse side of the cards suggests that the postcard industry was a profitable business as early as 1900. Both well-known international firms and local firms were engaged in the business. The names which appear frequently on postcards include John Little & Co, Tuck's Post Card, Max Hickles, Kelly Walsh Ltd, Arthur Dixon of the Isle of Wight, C.A. Ribiero, Hartwig & Co and M. Sternberg. Other brand names are G.H. Kiat, Koh and Co, Kong Hing Chiong & Co, Methodist Publishing House and M.S. Nakajima.

There are a handful of postcards on these pages displaying the name of G.R. Lambert who had a large photographic business in Singapore in the late 19th and early 20th century. In the book, *Twentieth Century Impressions of British Malaya* published in 1908 this description was given of the firm's business

"Lambert has maintained a high reputation for artistic portraiture, and of landscapes they have one of the finest collections in the East, comprising about three thousand subjects relating to Siam, Singapore, Borneo, Malaya and China. An extensive trade is done in picture postcards, the turnover being about a quarter of a million cards a year. A large stock of apparatus for amateurs is always kept in hand."

For this exhibition, the second of postcards organized by the National Archives, and in this book, we have concentrated on postcards printed in the first three decades of this century. By 1900 Singapore was fast becoming one of the busiest ports in the world. Founded by Sir Thomas Stamford Raffles in 1819, modern Singapore began as a commercial outpost of the British East India Company to further the Company's China trade and counter Dutch influence in Southeast Asia.

Raffles himself spent little time in Singapore and it was left to the first two Residents, Colonel William Farquhar (1819 – 1823) and John Crawford (1823–26) to realize his dream of Singapore's becoming "The Pride and Emporium of the East." The infant settlement grew quickly and the first census in 1824 tallied a population of 11,000. By 1871 the population had risen to 97,000 and by 1900 to 228,000. The dramatic increases were due to immigration, as the female population, especially among the Chinese, was extremely small.

Most of the immigrants settled in areas that had been prescribed for them in the original 1823 Town Plan outlined by Raffles. The plan put the government offices on the North bank of the river, the commercial activity on the South bank. The Chinese settled in what remains the old Chinatown area while the village of the Temenggong (the local chieftain who had signed the original treaty with Raffles) on the North bank was moved south between Tanjong Pagar and Telok Blangah.

Up until 1902 messages could only
be written on the front of postcards.
Montages combining several scenes
were popular.

The transformation of Collyer Quay
1900 to 1935, as seen in postcards.

Singapore. Johnston's Pier.

VIEW TAKEN FROM SEA, SINGAPORE

Collyer Quay, Singapore.

CLIFFORD PIER SINGAPORE

Raffles Place is another area that
has witnessed enormous changes to
the skyline as these four postcards,
circa 1900 to 1935, illustrate.

Raffles Place, Singapore.

H. No. 259 Raffles Square Singapore

SINGAPOUR. - Allée du Change

Other Malays settled in Kampong Malacca, Kampong Bencoolen and in the southern islands. Arabs and Bugis were allotted land in Kampong Glam; Hindu Indians in High Street; and the small number of Europeans began to occupy the area of River Valley Road, Orchard Road and Tanglin.

The Singapore Chinese were a heterogeneous people arriving from different provinces of China. They spoke different dialects (mainly Hokkien, Cantonese and Teochew), and were merchants, planters, artisans, and "coolies" (a word of Indian origin) who laboured in a wide range of occupations. There were also the Straits-born Chinese, referred to as a Nyonya if female, or as a Baba if male. These descendants of Chinese men who had taken Malay wives in the earlier settlements of Malacca and Penang had maintained their own unique customs and lifestyle. Under a naturalisation law passed in 1852 they had become British subjects. Although a minority, they were often wealthy and influential.

Malays made up three-fifths of Singapore's population in the census of 1824. By 1901, following the influx of Chinese and Indian immigrants, the 36,080 Malays represented slightly less than 16 percent of the population. Many were peninsular Malays, while others had come from Acheh, Bawean, Java and Sulawesi. They worked mostly as boatmen, fishermen, woodcutters, carpenters and *syces* or drivers. Expansion of the town and development of the harbour saw the development of new Malay settlements at Kampong Melayu, Geylang Serai and Pasir Panjang. Despite these disruptions, the Malays clung to their traditional lifestyle — their mode of dress, their style of housing, and their religion.

The Indians, less than 10 percent of Singapore's population in 1845, were by 1860 almost 16 percent, due to the influx of labourers and convicts. But in 1901, with almost 18,000 Indians in Singapore, they comprised only a little more than eight percent of the population, a percentage that has remained virtually constant. Those who came to Singapore during the 19th century were garrison troops, camp followers, labourers and convicts. Later immigrants were traders, businessmen, clerks and so on. Indian traders still dominate the textile trade in the High Street area, while many Punjabis and Sikhs continue to work as clerks, policemen and *jagas* or watchmen.

Postcards document history. The Oriental Hotel, once a fixture along Bras Basah Road, became the Japanese Commercial Museum.

Europeans have always been a small minority in Singapore's racial mix. They numbered only 94 in 1827. In 1860 there were still less than 500 and although their numbers doubled between 1901 and 1931 to somewhere over 8,000, they were still numerically insignificant. Most of the British were employed by the Colonial Civil Service. The remainder — along with Germans, Danes, Swiss, French, Dutch and Americans — were engaged in business.

The manufacturers of the picture postcards seen on these pages concentrated on two major themes — the modern and the picturesque. In 1905 the "modern" included the newly introduced electric trams and the just completed Hotel de L'Europe Building and Victoria Memorial Hall while the picturesque included bullock carts, jinrickshas, kampongs, Chinatown and hawkers.

The basic Town Plan outlined by Raffles and depicted in many of these postcards has altered little even to this day. Reclamation projects such as the levelling of Mount Wallich to fill the Telok Ayer basin, begun in 1879, added new roads to the original town plan, and the building of more bridges across the river improved communication. Today what has changed dramatically are the buildings on the grid and with urbanization, the rural landscape. Modest commercial structures and shophouses in many areas have given way to highrise towers. More recently, whole city blocks have been demolished to enable the building of the underground mass rapid transit system. Outlying areas that were for decades mangrove swamps, vegetable gardens and kampongs have been transformed into New Towns built by the Housing and Development Board. Still, some familiar landmarks remain.

Singapore has, in fact, experienced three building booms. The first coincided with the transfer of the Government of the Straits Settlements from India to direct rule from the Colonial Office in London in 1867, and the opening of the Suez Canal in 1869. The second began in the early 1900s and peaked in the mid-1920s while the third began to gather momentum in the early 1970s and subsided in the mid-1980s. Certainly the hobby of collecting old postcards has been given added impetus by urban renewal and the change in people's lifestyles.

In Singapore the recent collecting of pre-war postcards for their intrinsic value began as a spinoff of stamp collecting. Stamp collectors were more interested in the postmarks and the stamps affixed. The value of the postcard depended on such things rather than on the visual image. Only in the last decade or so have Singaporeans started to collect old postcards for their own merits. Cosmetically treated, they are being used for calendars and as book illustrations. Because of the dearth of pictorial materials depicting old Singapore, the National Archives has begun its own postcard collection. We have found this visual documentation an important way of promoting awareness of our own history.

This exhibition and this book bring together the best of the Archives' collection of picture postcards published circa 1900 – 1930. We hope they will make people aware of the historic value of postcards. If you should come upon old picture postcards don't discard them. Contact us, we will be delighted to have them!

Lily Tan (Mrs) *Director, National Archives*

An early view of the National Museum and a postcard embellished by the sender.

1 **Government House (Istana)** c1890s

Designed by J.F.A. McNair and built between 1876 and 1869 by Indian convict labourers, the Istana is today the official residence of the President of Singapore. From 1869 until 1959 the well-proportioned building was home to the British Governor of the Straits Settlements.

Panorama von Singapore.

2 **View of the City** c1890s

This early panoramic view of the city looks down from Mount Sophia towards Bras Basah Road area. In the background the steeples of three Christian churches can be clearly seen; from left, the Church of St. Peter and St. Paul, the Cathedral of the Good Shepherd and St. Andrew's Cathedral. All are still standing.

Singapore. Esplanade.

3 **Esplanade (Padang)** c1890s

This lush green space that once faced the sea has stood witness to most of Singapore's history. Originally called the Plain, English and Indian troops were quartered here after the founding of modern Singapore in 1819. The name was later changed to Padang, the Malay word for a recreational or sports ground. The field and its seafront (before it was reclaimed) made up the Esplanade, once the favourite venue for evening promenades. At the far end of the lawn is the early Cricket Club pavilion. No keeping off the grass here. Cricket, lawn tennis and other sports continue to be played on many evenings.

(22)   Statue of Sir Stamford Raffles, Singapore.

4 Raffles Statue c1905

Arms folded, head slightly bent and gazing thoughtfully to the sea, this bronze statue of Singapore's founder was unveiled on June 27, 1887 on the Padang. Raffles was born in 1781 on a ship off Jamaica. He joined the East India Company in London as a clerk at the age of 14. Posted to Penang as Assistant Secretary in 1805, he later became Lieutenant-Governor of Bencoolen. On January 29, 1819 Raffles signed a treaty with the Sultan of Johore and the Temenggong which granted the British the right to establish a trading station on the island. In 1823 he declared Singapore a free port. He died in England in 1826. The statue now stands near Victorial Memorial Hall.

S. C. C. Singapore.

5 Singapore Cricket Club c1920

Established in 1852 with only 28 members, the Cricket Club has catered to sportsmen for over 130 years. The first clubhouse was a simple structure at the western corner of the Esplanade. Subsequent clubhouses were built in 1877 and in 1884. The present clubhouse, seen here, was constructed in 1906 around the 1884 pavilion. By 1914 the club had almost 900 members and in the 1920s two more wings were added to the building. The Cricket Club, together with the Singapore Recreation Club at the opposite end of the Padang, are responsible for the maintenance of the lawn.

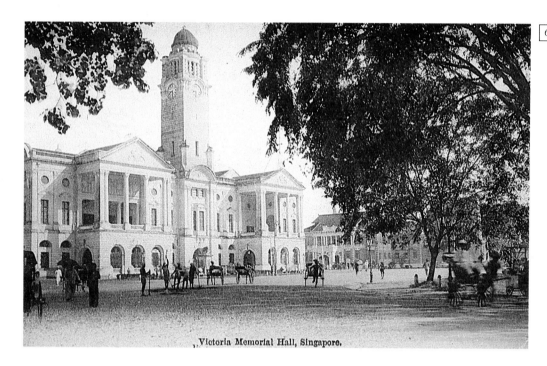

Victoria Memorial Hall, Singapore.

6 Victoria Theatre and Memorial Hall c1910

The theatre (the section of the building on the left) was built as a Town Hall in 1856–62 and provided space for offices, a stage and meeting hall. When the community decided to build a new theatre to commemorate the Jubilee celebrations of Queen Victoria, architects Swan and Maclaren integrated a new hall with the refaced existing building and joined the two with a 60 metre clock tower. Ground was broken in 1902. Upon completion in 1906 the building — a hybrid of Classical and Renaissance elements adapted to suit the tropical climate — became a civic landmark and so it has remained. The clock was installed in 1906.

Supreme Court, Singapore.

7 Old Court House (Parliament House) c1910

John Argyle Maxwell, a wealthy merchant in Java and appointed one of the first three magistrates by his friend Raffles in 1823, had this built as his private residence. Designed by Singapore's first important architect, G.D. Coleman, it remained unoccupied because of a dispute over the legal right to the land on which it was built. After completion in 1827 Maxwell leased it to the government. When the present Supreme Court was built on St. Andrews Road in 1939 the building became semi-derelict. It was given a new lease of life as the Assembly House in the 1950s and is now Parliament House.

8 Cavenagh Bridge c1905

Constructed by P.W. Maclellen of Glasgow in 1869, Cavenagh Bridge was assembled by convict labourers — the last major project undertaken by convict labour here. First called Edinburgh Bridge to commemorate the 1869 visit of the Duke of Edinburgh, the name was later changed to Cavenagh Bridge after Governor W.O. Cavenagh. Built to link the government offices in Empress Place with Commercial Square (Raffles Place), it was reduced to the status of a footbridge in 1909 when nearby Anderson Bridge opened. The sign prohibiting bullock carts, horses and heavy vehicles from crossing it remains to this day.

Cavanagh Bridge and General Post Office, Singapore.   No. 3

9 Fullerton Square c1910

This important triangular shaped square at the junction of Battery Road, Collyer Quay and Flint Street was named after Robert Fullerton, the first Governor of the Straits Settlements, 1826–28. On the right are the General Post Office and the Exchange Building. The columns on the left belong to the Hongkong and Shanghai Bank Building. The square is today a carpark.

10 **General Post Office** 1910

Called by novelist Joseph Conrad "The most important Post Office in the East", the GPO Building was built in 1874 on the site of Fort Fullerton. The building was demolished in the mid-1920s to make way for the recently renovated Fullerton Building which today houses the General Post Office and other government offices.

Jonston Pier, Singapore.   No. 1

11 **Johnston's Pier** c1905

Johnston's Pier, built in 1855 and named after Alexander Lawrie Johnston, was the main city landing point until its demolition in 1933. In the foreground are the small vessels which ferried passengers to and from vessels anchored in the harbour. A Scotsman, Johnston settled in Singapore in 1820, founded the firm of A.L. Johnston and Co, and remained the doyen of the European mercantile community until his retirement in 1841 from Singapore. His firm went out of business in 1892. The pier was torn down in 1933 to make way for the modern facility of Clifford Pier.

Battery Road, Singapore.

Battery Road c1905

Busy and crowded with traffic during most of the day, Battery Road was one of the main thoroughfares of the city. Carriages, hackney gharries, bullock carts and jinrickshas regularly plied this short stretch of road which links Raffles Place with Fullerton Square. The fountain, surrounded by trees, was a station for gharries waiting for hire. This view looks down Battery Road towards Raffles Place. On the left are the Hongkong and Shanghai Bank Building, The Medical Hall and Gresham House. The medical hall was demolished in the 1970s. In Chinese, Battery Road is called *Thor Khor An* which means "At the back of the European firms' godowns."

(27)   Hongkong & Shanghai Bank, Singapore.

13 **Hongkong and Shanghai Bank Building** c1910

In the early 1900s most banking business was in the hands of three British banks — The Chartered Bank of India, Australia and China, the Hongkong and Shanghai Banking Corporation and the Mercantile Bank of India. The first Chinese bank, the Kwong Yik Bank, opened in 1903. The ornate Hongkong and Shanghai Bank Building was a prominent landmark. Built in 1892, it was demolished in 1919 to make way for a larger, more modern structure. Founded in the 1860s in Hongkong, the bank was dubbed *Wayfoong* or "Abundance of Remittances" by the Chinese.

Finlayson Green, Singapore   × Our offices & godowns.   27/11/07

14 Finalyson Green 1907

Named after John Finlayson, Chairman of the Tanjong Pagar Dock Co in the 1880s, this patch of green still stands between Raffles Quay and Collyer Quay. The old office of the Straits Times at the end of Cecil Street can be seen in the background. Established in 1845 in Commercial Square, the Straits Times moved to Cecil Street in 1903. The buildings around the green housed mainly insurance and shipping companies.

Collyer Quay, Singapore.

15 Collyer Quay 1910

Collyer Quay was completed in 1864 and named after Col. C.C. Collyer who reclaimed part of the seafront using convict labourers. This shows, on the left, the offices of Behn Meyer and on the right the first Ocean Building, completed in 1864 and demolished in 1919 to make way for the second Ocean Building, completed in 1923. This was in turn demolished in 1969. The Quay together with Battery Road, Raffles Place and the streets leading into it formed the nucleus of the business activity of town. To the right on the postcard is Finlayson Green.

South Boatquay.

16 **South Boat Quay** c1900

From the start the river was the focal point of trading activities. In 1819 the river was a refuge for sampans serving as houseboats for the *orang laut* or sea pirates but these soon gave way to sailing lighters brought from southern India by the East India Company. The sheltered river banks made excellent landing and unloading places and merchants built offices, godowns and jetties for easier loading and unloading. The bullock carts lined up along the river's edge were commonly used for the transportation of goods over short distances. The ornate Bonham Building on the left stood at the corner of Chulia Street and Boat Quay.

Singapore River.

17 **Singapore River** c1912

Vessels crowd the river mouth. By the 1840s the population of the river consisted entirely of lightermen and their lighters following the development of the river as the main commercial centre, with a supplementary trading area at the estuary of the Rochor and Kallang Rivers. Cavenagh and Anderson bridges can be seen beyond. Anderson Bridge, built in 1909, is 100 metres closer to the river mouth and higher than Cavenagh Bridge. In 1983 the river vessels moved to a new location in Pasir Panjang.

Singapore. Boat Quay. *Thanks very much for letter. You observe 'the ricksha' in the picture; they find me a small trifle when I get in them. Tram suits C.R.N.* 56

18 Boat Quay c1905

On the far left is the present day Parliament House. The covered landing stage jutting out into the water in front of it was the site of the Hallpike Boatyard where boat repairs were carried out from 1823 until the 1860s. The crescent-shaped bank of South Boat Quay, with the ornate three-storey Bonham Building (now the site of the United Overseas Bank Building), stretches beyond. The swampy land along South Boat Quay was filled in with earth taken from a hillock ordered levelled by Raffles in 1823 in order to create the Commercial Square.

Singapore. *Dear M. this is a canal that runs through here it is a very busy spot boats are continually on the go* 6.12.04 63

19 Singapore River c1904

Tongkangs and *twakows*, the lighters which ferried goods from sea-going vessels to river godowns, are anchored along the river edge in this view looking south. Read Bridge in the foreground crosses the river near the uppermost limit of Boat Quay. Reconstructed in 1889, it was named after a prominent Scottish businessman William Henry Read. From the 1840s warehouses and godowns dominated the river banks.

Singapore

20 Mouth of the Singapore River
c1910

A picture which has graced many a postcard over the years. The scene takes in the mouth of the Singapore River with Cavenagh Bridge in the foreground and Anderson Bridge beyond as well as the government offices at Empress Place, Victoria Memorial Hall, the Cricket Club and the Padang beyond.

SINGAPORE RIVER & DRILL HALL

21 Singapore River and Drill Hall
c1905

The area around the mouth of the Singapore river saw demolitions, rebuilding and land reclamation, although the silhouette of buildings along the rest of the river remained basically unchanged from the 1880s until past the middle of this century. The Drill Hall shown here was designed by Major McCullum and built by the government for the Singapore Volunteer Artillery in 1891 on the site of the original fort on the island, Fort Fullerton. It stood for less than 20 years at the mouth of the river. Around 1907 it was dismantled and re-erected on reclaimed land at Beach Road not far from the Raffles Hotel.

Singapore. Boat Quay.

22 **Boat Quay** c1900

This shows Clarke Quay and Read Bridge. The godowns in the background testify to the immense business done along the river. Although Singapore possessed virtually no natural resources and produced no manufactured goods, within five years of its founding the settlement's exports amounted to six million Spanish dollars. As a market for the produce of the region and the merchandise of India, China and Europe, Singapore had already established itself as the entrepôt port of the region — a role it served for more than a hundred years. The building to the left of the bridge and the row of houses on the right were still standing in 1986.

Singapore. Boat Quay.

23 **South Boat Quay** c1900

A river choked by craft. In the 1860s three-quarters of all shipping business was done in Boat Quay. With the advent of the steamer in the 1860s seaside wharves were demanded for faster cargo handling and the shipping business shifted to facilities at Keppel Harbour. When shipping demands exceeded wharf space available, river traffic recovered as goods were hauled overland to Boat Quay for storage and distribution and by the 1880s the river was once again an important trade artery.

Raffles Place, Singapore

24 **Raffles Place** c1890s

An early view of the northern side of Raffles Place. Originally called Commercial Square, the plaza was built in 1823–24 on direct orders from Raffles and it initially developed as an adjunct to Boat Quay. Buildings on the Square's seaward side had their own jetties until reclamation of the Collyer Quay waterfront got underway in the 1860s. The Gemmill Fountain, erected in 1864 by auctioneer John Gemmill, is visible by the bullock cart. It is now in the grounds of the National Museum. The shophouse on the far right at the corner of Kling (now Chulia) Street and Raffles Place was destroyed by fire around 1970. Horses were auctioned here until 1886.

Singapore. Raffles Place.

25 **Raffles Place** c1900

The commercial and retail sections of town were not as divided as they are today and bustling Raffles Place was bordered by banks, offices as well as popular shopping emporia. The building on the far right was the first arcade; the building next to it housed the department store Robinson and Co, a noteworthy feature of Raffles Place from 1858 until it moved to Orchard Road in the early 1970s.

Singapore. Raffles Square.

26 **Raffles Place** 1901

Buildings in Raffles Square were decorated for the coronation of Edward VII in January 1901. In 1908 the Square was described as the great rendezvous of the European section of the community "and a very busy place from nine o'clock in the morning until five o'clock in the afternoon, after which hour, however, it is almost as deserted as the Sahara. In the daytime, the never ceasing stream of traffic — carriages, gharries, rickshas and foot passengers, with their wealth of colour, quaintness and movement — makes a wonderfully interesting kaleidoscopic procession."

Singapore. Commercial Centre.

27 **Bonham Building** c1906

This postcard shows the ornate Bonham Building in Raffles Place. Constructed in 1902 it was demolished in 1970 to make way for the Overseas Union Bank Building. The company Katz Brothers was formed in 1865. From shopkeepers, they launched into the importing and wholesale business. During World War I they closed their handsome retail store owing to the difficulties of getting new stock. The dispensary on the right was the equivalent of an American drugstore or British pharmacy.

Beach Road, Singapore

28 Beach Road c1905

For many years Beach Road ran parallel to the seashore. It formed, together with Robinson Road, Collyer Quay and the Esplanade one of the main east-west arteries of the town. The three-storey building in the photograph, just down the road from Raffles Hotel between Peck Seah Street and Purvis Street, has Palladian-style windows and is a classic example of turn-of-the-century urban architecture. Although it has been demolished, the three-storey building further down the road is still standing.

North Bridge Road, Singapore.

29 North Bridge Road c1915

North and South Bridge Road, connected by Elgin Bridge, formed another of the town's main east-west arteries. The building on the right is Meyer's Mansions which stood at the Coleman Street corner and housed among others the establishment of Messrs. Sun and Co, a photographic firm that specialized as outdoor photographers. Among the attractions of their stock were "many charming views of Singapore and Malaya which they have for sale," according to a 1922 description of the firm.

30 | **Hylam Street** c1915

Hylam Street runs between Middle Road and Bugis Street and the area once catered to Japanese residents. A Japanese kite can be seen flying on the left. The corner shop on the right was run by S.T. Yamato, photographer. Note the automobile on the street. Singapore's first car was imported in 1896 for Charles Burton Buckley, a prominent English resident.

31 | **Jalan Besar** c1920

Jalan Besar was extended and widened in the 1890s. In the first decade of this century the swampy, flood-prone area to the north towards Lavender Street was drained and the side roads developed or extended. The tannery industry flourished on the south side of the road. Many of the shophouses lining the street were built in the early 1900s. By the 1920s visitors were already remarking on the town's traffic congestion. One observer commented that the roads "were never built for the demands of today, and to widen them is, with the heights to which land values have reached, quite impractical save in small degree here and there."

Singapore. Main Road.

32 **Singapore Main Road** c1890

This postcard shows the quarters of the Tanjong Pagar Dock Company along a road leading to the entrance of the company. Guthrie Hill is in the background of this photograph taken around 1892. The Tanjong Pagar Dock Company was one of the largest companies in the business of providing wharves for cargo handling, repairing ships and constructing small vessels. It gradually swallowed up its smaller rivals and in 1905 ownership was transferred to the publicly owned Tanjong Pagar Dock Board.

Singapore. Selegie Road.

33 **Selegie Road** c1910

This postcard shows Selegie Road at its junction with Prinsep Street. The shophouses on the right survive, although they are in a very dilapidated condition.

Newton Station, Singapore.

34 Newton Station c1910

From the Tank Road station passengers travelled via Oxley Hill and across Orchard Road to Newton Station then north to the Woodlands Station. The railway was built in the first years of this century with government funds, but only after much debate. In 1909 the line that linked Singapore to the Malayan hinterland was completed. To the left of the tracks shown here ran the Bukit Timah canal.

(27)   Hackney and hackney jinrikisha police, Singapore.

35 Hackney c1910

Smaller carriages known as hackneys or gharries crowded the streets of the business quarter of the town. Tourists could hire a hackney from Abrams' Horse Repository on Orchard Road or Dallan's Australian Horse Repository on Koek Road. "Daddy" Abrams accomodated 250 animals, and was influential in the local social life and contributed a historic part to local racing before his death in 1911. Most hackney drivers were Malays and Indians. Rules stated that "no driver shall be required to drive one pony a greater distance than ten miles or remain engaged for more than nine hours at a time."

HILL STREET SINGAPORE

36 **Hill Street** c1920

This view of Hill Street from Coleman Street illustrates the various modes of transport used in the 1920s. By 1920 there were around 5,000 motor cars, hundreds of motor lorries and motorcycles clogging roads, the chaos made worse by tramcars, motorcycles, rickshas, bullock carts and handcarts. Hill Street cuts through the lower slope of Fort Canning Hill. The Chinese call it *One Ke Swa Ka*, meaning "At the foot of the Governor's House." The tower of the Hill Street Fire Station, erected in 1909, is visible down the street on the left. In the left foreground is the corner of Hill Street and River Valley Road where the Hill Street Building stands.

Coleman Street, Singapore

37 **Coleman Street** c1910

This view looks south down Coleman Street towards the sea. On the right is the Adelphi Hotel Building, opened in 1906 and run by the Sarkies Brothers who also owned and operated Raffles Hotel. On the left are the grounds of St. Andrews Cathedral. The road is named after C.D. Coleman the Irish architect who made his home in Singapore from 1826 until his death in 1844 and who designed many important buildings. He combined his private practice with a government job and was first Overseer of Convicts and Superintendent of Public Works. Coleman built his own house further up the street where a shopping centre now stands.

H. No. 275 Stamford Road Singapore

38 Stamford Road c1915

Stamford Road takes the second name of the island's founder. The Chinese call it *Lau Chooi Koei*, "Flowing Water Road" because it was built along the banks of the Sungei Bras Basah, the rivulet which flowed from Orchard Road to the sea and is the present-day Stamford Canal. This view shows the Methodist Publishing House Building, built in 1908 at the corner of Stamford Road and Armenian Street. It is still used as a bookshop.

GHAUT SINGAPORE.

39 Dhoby Ghaut c1915

Indian *dhobies* (laundry men) once washed the clothes of residents in the stream which ran down from Orchard Road to the sea and dried them on the open space seen to the right of the postcard. The Presbyterian Church (at left) was erected in 1879 and recently modernized. Beyond is Mount Sophia. The same view today would show a park where the row of shophouses stands and the Cathay Cinema and Cathay Building further down where the domed building is visible through the trees.

33

Bras Basah Road,
Singapore

40 **Brash Basah Road** c1905

Brash Basah Road runs parallel to Stamford Road and is so called because in the early days wet rice — *bras basah* in Malay — was exposed to the sun on the banks of the Sungai Bras Basah, now known as Stamford Canal. The road was also called Church Street and College Street because of the large number of schools and churches in the vicinity. This postcard shows the northern end of the road at the junction with Dhoby Ghaut. In the center is the Lois Molteni Confectionery, a popular place, judging by the number of vehicles waiting for customers outside. The site is presently occupied by the Cathay Cinema Building.

SINGAPORE — CONVENT — *Entrance*

41 **Entrance to the Convent of the Holy Infant Jesus** c1905

Located at the corner of Bras Basah Road and Victoria Street, this education facility for girls was opened in 1854 by Father Beurel. By the turn of the century it included an orphanage and a refuge for distressed women irrespective of race. The original building was a private residence designed by G.D. Coleman in 1834, the shutters of which are visible on the right. Over the years the facilities expanded until the school covered an entire block. The school moved to new premises in Toa Payoh and a portion of the grounds were taken over for the construction of the Mass Rapid Transit system.

Anglo-Chinese School, Singapore.

42 **Anglo-Chinese School** c1890

Opened in March 1886 by a Methodist, Rev. W.F. Oldham, at Amoy Street, it was moved in November 1886 to the foot of Fort Canning in what is now Canning Rise. The new building was opened in 1893. During the Japanese Occupation, the school was taken over by the Japanese. In 1959 a new three-storey building was opened on this site. The message on the card reads "Guy taught here."

Singapore. St. Joseph Institution.

43 **St Joseph's Institution** c1900

One of several schools along Bras Basah Road, this Catholic boys' school was founded in 1852 by Father Beurel, a French Jesuit priest. The centre section of the building was designed by Brother Lothaire and opened in 1867. The wings, designed by Father Nain, were added around 1900. The collonade offered a cool sheltered space for generations of schoolboys. The school will move to new quarters soon.

44 **Raffles Institution** c1910

It was Sir Stamford Raffles' dream to cater for formal education in Singapore. Despite many obstacles he laid the foundation stone in 1823 of an educational institution "for the cultivation of Asian languages, the education of the sons of Malay rulers and the moral and intellectual improvement of the peoples of Asia." The building seen here is largely the work of G.D. Coleman who renovated the original building in 1835–37. The three-storey block adjoining Bras Basah Road was built in 1875–76. In 1967 the school was declared unsafe. Several years later it moved to new premises at Grange Road. The building was demolished to make way for Raffles City.

Raffles Museum & Library, Singapore.

45 **Raffles Museum (National Museum)** c1910

In 1849 it was decided to form a museum with a view to collecting historical and archaeological objects. The collection was housed in Raffles Institution and the Town Hall before this Victorian-style building was opened in October, 1887. The building was later expanded and today it houses a collection which includes modern art, jade, ceramics, ethnographic material and Singapore memorabilia.

Singapore.

St. Andrews Cathedral, Singapore.

46 **Chapel, Convent of the Holy Infant Jesus** c1911

The French Gothic Revival style chapel with buttresses, fine leaded stained glass windows and a splendid Gothic Arcade was built in 1910 with donations from the public. Although the school has moved to premises in Toa Payoh from the site the chapel still stands.

47 **St Andrews Cathedral** 1908

The original Anglican Church was built in 1835–36 by G.D. Coleman on land set aside by the government near the Padang. In 1855 it was demolished, after being declared unsafe. Under Major J.F.A. McNair and a crew of convict labourers the present church took shape. The Gothic Revival structure was consecrated in 1861. In 1973 it was gazetted a National Monument.

Victoria Street, Singapore.

48 **Victoria Street** c1905

This view shows Victoria Street at its junction with Stamford Road. Part of the Hotel Van Wijk can be seen on the right.

Electric Tram, Singapore.

49 **Electric Tram** 1910

In 1902 the Municipal Authority passed the Tramway Ordinance giving Singapore Electric Tramways Ltd an exclusive right to run the tramways. The first car made its appearance on July 25, 1905. But the company was never financially successful. It was liquidated in 1922 and brought over by the Shanghai Electric and Construction Co. Trams ran until 1927. At the height of their service they daily carried over 10,000 passengers on the six lines.

38

Sophia Road, Singapore.

50 **Sophia Road** c1905

A jinricksha puller labours down Sophia Road while another one pauses to rest. Jinricksha pullers had to be licensed but vehicle owners often by-passed the regulations. Exploited pullers were forced to work long hours and licence badges were transferred indiscriminately. Inexperienced pullers, newly arrived from China and ill-equipped to handle heavy city traffic, provided the cheapest labour source.

PARK ROAD, SINGAPORE

51 **Park Road** c1905

Peoples Park in 1905 provided a refreshing retreat to Chinatown residents who lived in dark, stuffy cubicles. The area bounded by New Bridge Road, Park Road and the foot of Pearl's Hill lives on in the name of the shopping complex built nearby around 1970.

North Bridge Road, Singapore.

Street Scene, Singapore.

52 **North Bridge Road** c1910

This postcard captures a classic Singapore town scene of rows of shophouses where Colombo Court now stands. To the Chinese, the area north of Elgin Bridge is *Seoh poh* meaning "small town"; the area south is *Two poh* or "big town".

53 **High Street** c1915

This postcard shows the corner of North Bridge Road looking south down High Street towards Empress Place. The street was so named because the slopes of Fort Canning Hill once extended down to Empress Place. By 1900 High Street was one of the main shopping areas. Visitors were recommended to inspect the shops here but warned that "the price asked for an article is usually treble the amount that will ultimately be accepted."

A Chinese Residence, Singapore.

Straits Chinese Recreation Club, Singapore.

54 **Chinese House** c1910

This residential terrace house along Neil Road is typical of the architecture favoured by the well-to-do Straits Chinese during the late 19th and early 20th century. Such houses — dubbed Chinese Baroque, Palladian Chinese or Straits Chinese architecture — are an eclectic combination of Chinese, Malay and European Classical details. Until World War II the terrace house dominated domestic architecture. The standard floor plans were given variation in the the treatment of details. Ornate facades such as this can still be seen on established streets.

55 **Straits Chinese Recreation Club Pavilion** c1910

This octagonal pavilion stood in the middle of Hong Lim Green in Chinatown for many years. The club was formed in 1885 and offered facilities for tennis, billiards, cricket and hockey.

Orchard Road, Singapore.

56 **Orchard Road** c1900

A lone bullock cart takes a quiet stroll down Orchard Road in the days before the commercial explosion of the road. Once part of a plantation run by Willam Cuppage in the late 1830s, by the 1850s the Orchard Road and Tanglin areas had become increasingly popular as a residential area because of the good roads and the prettier approach to town.

Orchard Road, SINGAPORE.

57 **Orchard Road** c1910

The view in this postcard looks south from the junction of Cairnhill Road, marked on the left by the gaslight. By now the road's commercial character was more established.

58 **Orchard Road** c1913

This view looks north and shows the Orchard Road Railway Bridge near Emerald Hill. From 1903 until 1932 trains ran from the Tank Road railway station across this bridge to the Woodlands Jetty.

59 **Orchard Road** c1930

On the left is Amber Mansions, completed in 1922 and demolished recently for work on a Mass Rapid Transit station.

60

Singapore. Botanic Garden.

24/10/08 Do you intend to stop exchanging with correspondents in the Straits, or do you prefer cards other than of the Straits? Kindly explain. V. Jarre

61

(57)   Botanical Garden, Singapore.

62

(49)   Botanical Garden, Singapore.

63

SINGAPORE, Botanical Garden

The Botanic Gardens c1900 – 1910

The Botanic Gardens as we know it today was established as a public park and experimental station for new crops in 1859 on land given by the Chinese pioneer Hoo Ah Kay, also known as Whampoa. (The Botanic Gardens set up on Canning Hill in 1822 was eventually disbanded). The Gardens were always a major tourist attraction and an early 20th century guidebook to Singapore advises "the visitor to Singapore will find no lack of objects of interest and beauty. One of the first sights that tourists generally make a point of viewing is the Botanical Gardens, among the loveliest institutions of the kind in the East."

Even then the gardens included a large variety of orchid and tropical ferns and plants, a strip of primeval jungle as well as the pond. In addition to providing scenic beauty, the garden carried on important research. H.N. "Mad" Ridley, Director of the Gardens between 1888 and 1912, imported a large number of orchids into Singapore and made a scientific inventory of them. His work in orchids was continued by later directors and staff. In 1877, the first Brazilian rubber seeds were sent from England to the Gardens but the potential of rubber was ignored until Ridley's arrival. By 1897 he had devised a method of tapping the tree without damaging the bark and for years he pressed coffee planters to grow rubber trees. But it wasn't until the popularity of automobiles that rubber became a major crop.

The rest is history.

Hotel de L'Europe, Singapore

64 **Hotel de L'Europe** c1910

For many years the hotel business centred around the Esplanade, High Street and Coleman Street. The L'Europe was at the centre of them all, the only hotel facing the Esplanade. Established in 1855 on the corner of High Street and Esplanade Road the vast building was built at a cost of one million dollars and opened in 1905. A 1905 advertisement boasts: "Magnificently furnished with elegant simplicity and modern in construction, offering every advantage and necessity conducive to comfort and health." In the early 1930s the hotel ran into financial difficulties. The government acquired the land in 1934 for the Supreme Court Building.

(76)
Hotel van Wijk, Singapore.

65 **Hotel Van Wijk** c1911

Located along Stamford Road between North Bridge Road and Victoria Street the Hotel Van Wijk was listed as one of the dozen or so principal hotels in town in the early years of this century. It was later incorporated into the grounds of the Convent of the Holy Infant Jesus. Guests crossed a small bridge over Stamford Canal.

The Cocoanut Palm, Singapore.

66 **Seaview Hotel** c1909

Established in the late 19th century in Katong, the Seaview Hotel with its scenic view and coconut palms was an ideal retreat for those seeking peace and quiet in a tranquil atmosphere.

Raffles Hotel - Singapore

RAFFLES HOTEL

67 **Raffles Hotel** c1900

Considered the hub of Singapore's social life in the 1900s, the Raffles continues to symbolise the magic and mystery of the Orient. Established by the Sarkies Brothers in 1887, this building, designed by the firm of Swan and Maclaren, opened in 1896. During the Japanese Occupation top ranking Japanese officers used the hotel as their residential quarters.

SARKIES BROS., PROPRIETORS.

THE PALM COURT, RAFFLES HOTEL, SINGAPORE.

68 **Palm Court, Raffles Hotel** c1920s

One of the most endearing features of the Raffles Hotel is the tropical garden space in the middle of the hotel compound.

69 **Sitting Room, Seaview Hotel**

This postcard gives an idea of trends in tropical interior decoration, circa 1900.

Dining Hall, sealing 300 persons   Adelphi Hotel, Singapore
G. R. Lambert & Co., Singapore

70 | **Dining Room, Adelphi Hotel**
c1910

Originally established in 1863 in Raffles Place, the Adelphi moved to High Street and finally to the junction of Coleman Street and North Bridge Road around 1905. The dining room had a seating capacity of 300 and an advertisement for the hotel in 1905 boasts: "The interior presents a palatial, imposing bright appearance with magnificent marble effects and sumptuous apartments". The building was torn down in the early 1970s.

DINING ROOM HOTEL EUROPE

71 | **Dining, Room Hotel de L'Europe**
c1910

An early 20th century visitor to Singapore passed this judgement on the L'Europe and its competitor the Raffles. "It is generally agreed that there is no choice between the Raffles and the Europe, both are good first class, comfortable hotels and the best you can find in the Orient … The food is quite good enough." A 1907 advertisement for the hotel claims "the finest Dining Room in the East. The Cuisine and Cellar are objects of special care."

Teutonia Club, Singapore

72 Teutonia Club (Goodwork Park Hotel) c1905

Built near the junction of Scotts Road and Stevens Roads, the Teutonia Club Building opened its doors to the German community for recreation and social life in September 1900. The club was founded in 1856 and the building was declared enemy property during World War I and seized by the government. Converted into a hotel in 1929, it was used as a residence for Japanese officers during World War II and later as a War Crimes Trial Court. The building resumed functioning as a hotel in 1947 and so it is today.

Grand stand, Race Course, Singapore.

73 Race Course c1905

The old Race Course was near Serangoon Road at what is now Farrer Park. A racing club had been established as early as 1843.

74 **Orchard Road Market** c1911

By the early 1900s there were five large markets in Singapore — Town Market at the western end of Raffles Quay; Clyde Terrace Market on Beach Road; Ellenborough Market near New Bridge Road; Rochor Market and the Orchard Road Market. It was built in 1891 on land acquired by the government from Edwin Koek, a solicitor. The brick gable facade was added in 1909. Municipal Architect A. Gordon remarked that as the market faced an important street, "it had been designed with an architectural front." The fountain was brought over from Telok Ayer Market in 1902. The market was demolished in 1978 and the stalls moved into Cuppage Centre.

New Market, Singapore.

75 **Ellenborough Market** c1910

Also known as New Market, it was built in 1891 on the site of an earlier market. In 1978 the hawkers were resettled in a new multi-storey building bearing the same name. It is affectionately known to locals as the "Teochew Market".

(28)   Jinrikisha stand, Singapore

76 **Jinricksha Stand** c1910

This popular form of transportation — the cheapest available — was imported from Japan via Shanghai in the 1880s and only faded out when the trishaw was introduced in 1947. Around the time the photograph on this postcard was taken, the fare was three cents for half a mile or less; or 20 cents for an hour.

Tank Road Railway Station, Singapore.

77 **Tank Road Railway Station** c1905

The Tank Road Railway Station served as the main terminus for passenger trains coming down from the Woodlands Jetty on the Singapore Kranji Railway. Parked outside are jinrickshas waiting for fares. Even in the early days taxi services were provided at transportation focal points. Opened in 1903, the station was closed in 1932 when the Keppel Road Station opened. Its land was leased to a school and converted into a sports field.

(33)   Seavenger and dust-van, Singapore

78 **Bullock Cart** c1910

In 1856 a Municipal Council was set up to take charge of public health, building and repairing roads and public building works. In 1887 a Municipal Ordinance was passed to cope with the rapid expansion of the town. The Conservancy Department (whose cart is shown here) was set up at that time.

(11)   Water-car, Singapore

79 **Bullock Watering Cart** c1910

Though a clumsy and inefficient vehicle, the bullock cart provided an essential service before motorisation was introduced. It was commonly used for the transportation of goods for short distances. This watering cart is posed along the Stamford Canal.

(97)   Kling Street, Singapore.

80 **Kling Street** c1910

The junction of Kling Street (now Chulia Street) and the northwest corner of Raffles Place was dominated for many years by the ornate Bonham building on the right.

Singapore. Court House.

81 **South Bridge Road** c1900

The scene on this postcard looking down South Bridge Road towards Tanjong Pagar shows the heavy traffic on South Bridge Road. On the left is the Police Headquarters and on the right the Police Court.

(66)
The Police Head Quarters, Singapore.

82 **Central Police Station** c1905

With the transfer of rule from India to the Colonial Office in London in 1869 the pace of construction of public buildings stepped up. Nearly all of Singapore's public buildings were designed by engineers in the Public Works Department or its earlier equivalents. The first central police station was built in 1887. A disasterous explosion occurred in the building's courtyard in 1891 killing several constables and severely injuring others. When the building was repaired, the Baroque-Islamic clock tower was added.

(10)
The Police Court, Singapole.

83 **Police Court** c1900

This imposing presence along South Bridge Road combined a Malay-style porch with a French mansard-style roof. The T-shaped building at the south end of Hong Lim Green was erected around 1884 and demolished in the 1970s.

Singapore. Chinatown. I.L 120

84 **Chinatown** 1890s

How Singapore came to have sepa-rate ethnic settlements is a well-told tale. In 1823 Raffles returned to Singapore after an absence of several years and was shocked at the chaos of his town. A Town Com-mittee was formed and Raffles re-commended to them that areas be specifically allocated to the various racial groups in order to create an orderly community and maintain peace. Chinatown took root on the southwest side of the Singapore River and by the 1840s·it was fairly developed with rows of single and two-storey shophouses. Although labelled Chinatown this view is actually of a street in Kampong Bahru, looking south to the sea.

New Bridge Road and its Bustling Communication, Singapore.   No. 1

85 **New Bridge Road** c1900

Characteristic of Chinatown were bullock carts and jinrickshas, the more humble means of transporta-tion. The fancier horse drawn car-riages were more often seen around Commercial Square (Raffles Place). Introduced in 1880, the jinricksha quickly became a distinctive feature of the Singapore street scene. After only eight years their numbers swel-led to 1,8000. Most of the early jinricksha pullers were immigrants who stayed in densely populated areas of Chinatown. The building on the right of this oft reproduced scene was still standing in 1986.

Hindu Temple, Singapore

86 Hindu Temple c1910

The gopuram of the Sri Mariam-man Temple has long been a familiar sight on South Bridge Road. The oldest Hindu temple in Singapore still in use, it was built in 1843 and has been a National Monument since 1973. Owing to the rise in population and increased commercial activities, many shop-houses along the road were re-built in the 1910s. An early 20th century visitor described the road this way: "Along its entire length, this street is lined with Chinese shops of all conceivable kinds — silver-smiths', ivory workers', rice shops, pork shops, eating houses, hotels and what not — whilst the side streets leading from it are simply thronged with stalls …"

Jinriksha Station, Singapore.

87 Jinricksha Station c1915

By the turn-of-the-century the in-flux of Chinese immigrants had caused an acute accommodation shortage in town. Rooms were partitioned into tiny cubicles and shacks were built in narrow court-yards and airwells.

88 **Trengganu Street** c1910

Often thought of as the heart of today's Chinatown, Trengganu Street is still graced by the three-storey shophouse building on the left. A less classical example of shophouse architecture, the building has an unusual overhanging third storey built in timber.

89 **Nagore Durgha** c1910

This Muslim Shrine, built in Telok Ayer Street in 1828–30 by South Indian Muslims, is a squared partly roofed enclosure surrounded by an ornate wall that is a mixture of East and West. Fluted Corinthian pillars and half moon fanlights on the lower level have little in common with the intricate work above. The Shrine was declared a National Monument in 1973.

58

Singapore. China Town.

90 Telok Ayer Street c1900

For many years Telok Ayer Street ran close to and parallel with the original seashore and formed the base of the Chinese settlement. Most of the boatyards and ships chandlers were located here and at Tanjong Rhu. One indication of the street's importance is the large number of religious and clan associations erected along the street in the early years, such as the Thian Hock Kheng temple, shown on the right. The temple was constructed circa 1842 with materials imported from China at considerable cost to the sponsoring businessmen, like Singapore pioneers Tan Kim Seng and Tan Tock Seng. In 1973 it was gazetted a National Monument.

Singapore. Entrance to a Chinese house.

91 Entrance to a Chinese House c1900

This mislabelled postcard is actually a photograph of the interior of the Wak Hai Cheng Bio on Phillip Street. Both a temple and a clan association, it was constructed in 1850 by the Teochew community. The building is still standing.

(7)   Chinese Protectorate, Singapore.

92 Chinese Protectorate c1900

An 1875 report on labour abuses concluded that the Colonial government knew little about the Chinese Community. Recommendations included establishing firmer control over the community with more official protection for immigrants. These findings led in 1877 to the establishment of a Chinese Protectorate. This building stood on Havelock Road until it was demolished in 1930. The Chinese Protectorate, which was at first housed in a Chinese shophouse on North Canal Road, dealt with the Chinese slave trade, secret societies, prostitution and other welfare issues.

Singapore. Hong Lim Green.
S. C. R. C.

93 Hong Lim Green c1900

A plot of land in Chinatown was offered by the Colonial government to the Chinese population as a recreation ground on the condition that it be properly kept. Cheang Hong Lim donated $3,000 in 1876 for the conversion of the space, in front of the Police Court, into a public garden which bears his name today. The pavilion of the Singapore Chinese Recreation Club can be seen in the postcard as well as the outline of the Police Court Building. Hong Lim Green is still one of the few open green spaces in densely populated Chinatown.

94 Neil Road c1905

Once a prestigious address for well-to-do families, Neil Road is still lined with some impressive Chinese residential terrace houses, although the buildings are in a dilapidated state. The building at the corner is the Jinricksha Station, built in 1903. The building still stands and looks very much the same today as in this postcard.

95 Anson Road c1900

The prominent three-storey building in the centre of the postcard is the Boustead Institute for Seamen built in 1892 with funds donated by the estate of Edward Boustead, the founder of Boustead's Trading Company in 1827. The Institute was meant to provide a "means of shelter, rest, recreation, amusement or intellectual cultivation of seamen." It was fitted with bedrooms, refreshment rooms and a meeting hall. It no longer stands.

Singapore, P. & O. Wharf,

96 **P. & O. Wharf** c1905

As port traffic increased so too did congestion in the Singapore River. The situation was aggravated in 1845 when the Eastern Steam Navigation Co. and the Peninsular & Oriental Steam Navigation Co. started the first scheduled steamship services through Singapore. By 1852 the P & O Co. had opened a wharf at New Harbour.

Singapore. Malay Village St. James.

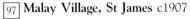

97 **Malay Village, St James** c1907

This postcard shows the houses on stilts of the *Orang Laut* (Sea Gypsies) off Pulau Brani. St James was a promontory lying between Blangah Bay and Sibert Bay. By 1926 both bays had been almost totally reclaimed and the original sites are now crossed by Keppel Road and Telok Blangah Road.

St. John's Island, Singapore.

98 **St John's Island** c1908

Island residents wait for the ferry.

Puloe Brani Ferry - Singapore

99 **Pulau Brani** c1905

Pulau Brani, inhabited mainly by *Orang Laut*, was also the site of Singapore's first modern industry, a tin smelter built on the island by the Straits Trading Company in 1890. In the background is Pulau Blakang Mati (Sentosa Island). Because of its sheltered position, Pulau Brani was used as a coaling depot for British naval vessels. The repair dock was built there in the 1860s.

Singapore. Keppel Harbour.

100 **Keppel Harbour** c1900

This postcard shows the entrance to the harbour, circa 1900. The building on the right is the Peninsula and Oriental Wharf, completed in 1852. During the 14th century, Chinese seafarers had discovered the Keppel Harbour channel. They called it "Dragon's Teeth Gate". William Farquhar, the first Resident of Singapore, referred to it as New Harbour in 1820 and the name was changed to Keppel Harbour in 1900.

Raffles Lighthouse, Singapore.

101 **Raffles Lighthouse**

Situated on Coney Island, Raffles Lighthouse stands at the entrance of the Straits of Malacca. The foundation stone was laid by Col. W.J. Butterworth on 24 May 1854 and it began operating the following year. The lighthouse is visible for about 12 nautical miles.

102 Tanjong Pagar Wharf c1905

In 1866 the Tanjong Pagar Dock Company opened for business with 230 metres of wharf space. The company expanded, opening docks and buying others, like the Borneo Wharf in 1885. By 1899 they completed their virtual control over the entire shipping business, operating five dry docks and having a wharf frontage of more than 2,000 metres. In 1912 the Singapore Harbour Board was constituted under the Straits Settlements Ports Ordinance. The government expropriated the Tanjong Pagar Dock Company and handed over control of its facilities to the Board, the precursar of the Port Authority of Singapore.

TANJONG PAGAR WHARF, SINGAPORE.

103 Disembarkment Wharf c1900

A first view of Singapore. Passengers disembarking after a long sea voyage were welcomed by busy scenes such as this.

Singapore — Le Wharf de débarquement

Singapore Chinese Woman.

104 **Straits Chinese Woman** c1905

This classic hand-tinted Nonya portrait, complete with studio props, shows the traditional *baju kurong*, the national costume of the Straits-born women until around the time of World War I when it was replaced by the more modern looking *sarong kebaya*. Nonyas were secluded from the age of puberty and prepared for serving their husbands and mothers-in-law in an arranged marriage. They spoke Malay and most were poorly educated.

Chinese Boy's School, Singapore.

105 **Chinese Boys' School** c1905

The Chinese Boys' School (Chinese Free School) in Amoy Street was established in 1854 and endowed by the wealthy philanthropist Tan Kim Seng. It was only one of dozens of small Chinese schools funded by wealthy merchants. Classes were in dialect and run along traditional Confucian lines. Standards varied considerably.

Grandma's joy.

106 **Grandma's Joy** c1900

A portrait of Straits Chinese children showing traditional dress and jewellery. Singapore's population grew more rapidly from immigration than from births, due to the small number of females here. For children, the early years of life were critical ones. In 1910 the child mortality rate was 345 per thousand. No wonder children were "joys".

Singapore. Malay Lady.

Singapore. Full dressed Chinese child.

107 **Malay Lady** c1900

By 1901 Singapore's Malay-Muslim population of more than 36,000 was a cosmopolitan mixture of immigrants and sojourners from Java, Sumatra, the peninsular states, from as far away as the Middle East and as close as the neighbouring islands. This beautiful woman is dressed in a *baju kurong* and bedecked in Malay silver ornaments. The black ribbon tied around her neck is a concession to European Victorian fashion.

108 **Straits Chinese Child** c1900

The Chinese costume worn in this portrait was reserved for special occasions such as the New Year or a Straits Chinese wedding ceremony. The elaborate headdress is a complicated network of silver filigree ornaments including phoenixes, peacocks, peonies, butterflies as well as Buddhist and Taoist symbols of blessing and good luck.

Singapore.

Singapore. Chinese actor.

109 **Indian Girl** c1900

Most of the thousands of Indian immigrants were males as Indian migration increased steadily from the mid-19th century to peak in the early 20th century. The migration of Indian women and children became common only after 1930. An Indian woman perhaps not unlike the girl in this portrait, was poetically described by the 19th century travel writer Isabella Bird as "a beautiful object, classical in form, exquisite in movement and artistic in colouring, a creation of the tropic sun."

110 **Opera Performer** c1900

Chinese street opera was the major form of entertainment for the Chinese community. Performances were sponsored by temple or clan associations on religious occasions, such as the birthday of a God or Goddess, or the Festival of Ghosts during the Seventh lunar month. The familiar classics, played out by actors such as this in splendid costumes and headdresses, helped to allay the homesickness of the coolies.

69

Kling hawker of breads and cakes, waiting for customers, Singapore.

(7) A Chinese street stall, Singapore

111 **Indian Cake and Bread Seller** c1910

Singapore Indians — called Klings during the early days — were a highly diverse community in terms of class, caste, language and religion, from chetty moneylenders, clerks and junior administrators in the colonial bureaucracy to cooks, messengers, shopkeepers, hack gharry *syces* and *dhoby* washermen. Those who settled in todays "Little India", the Serangoon Road area, were mostly commercial migrants.

112 **Chinese Street Stall** c1910

By the early 20th century Singapore was one of the most cosmopolitan societies in Asia. Nearly three-quarters of the population was Chinese with sizeable minorities of Indians, Ceylonese, Jews, Arabs, Eurasians, Malays, Sumatrans and Javanese. Visitors often remarked on the many languages spoken on the streets and the amazing parade of costumes. Many of the poorer inhabitants of the city lived in cramped, crowded and unhygienic quarters with no eating facilities. At rough wooden tables Chinese labourers could eat inexpensive meals.

Extension of original cutting on an old Para rubber

113 **H.N. Ridley** c1910

H.N. "Mad" Ridley poses with one of his rubber trees. The Director of Gardens and Forests, Straits Settlements 1888 – 1911, he devised a way to tap latex without destroying the tree. Singapore, despite its small size, had substantial rubber estates by 1910. The first rubber was grown commercially on the Trafalgar Coconut Plantation in Ponggol about 1907. By 1914 Malayan rubber exports accounted for half the world supply.

BEAUTIES OF THE EAST. SINGAPORE.

If these are beauties Lord help the ugly ones

114 **Beauties of the East** c1906

This group of young Straits-born Chinese women are wearing the *kasut manik* or beaded slippers that were so popular among the Nonyas. Women continued to be a minority well into this century. In 1911 men outnumbered women by eight to one.

Singapore. Malay Radjas.

Dear Ernie thanks very much for letter how would you like to be face to face with these people

115 **Malay Sultan** c1900

This photograph showing the Sultan of Perak seated under an umbrella and surrounded by his retinue conveys regal dignity. In 1895 the Federated Malay States were formed in the Peninsula. Each state was administered by a British Resident while matters pertaining to religion and customs were in the hands of the Sultans.

Opium Smoking

116 **Opium Smoking** c1900

Opium smoking crossed class barriers and was a pastime of both the rich and the poor. Revenue from the sale of opium was a financial mainstay of the Colonial government up to the 20th century. In the 19th century wealthy Chinese found the opium farm lucrative while European merchants were content to see the bulk of revenue levied on opium rather than on commerce, property or salaries. In 1910 the government, torn between financial and moral concerns, took over the manufacture and sale of opium. Up to the mid-1920s the sale of opium contributed nearly half of Singapore's revenue. The government manufactured it until World War II.

Chinese Girls' School.

117 **The Singapore Chinese Girls' School** c1905

In April 1899 a committee of Straits Chinese men formulated a bold scheme for instituting a school for the education of Chinese girls in Malay, Chinese and English, arithmetic, geography, music and sewing. The school opened in June with a mere seven girls and was beset by financial difficulties for some years. In 1908 a limited liability company was formed to run the school. The girls shown here are dressed in traditional Straits Chinese *baju kurong*. Look closely and you will see one male student, his hair in the long queue worn before the demise of the Manchu dynasty in 1911.

118 **Wayang Performance** c1900

The Malay word *wayang* or "shadow" evolved to mean any form of theatrical representation. In Singapore it has long been synonymous with Chinese street opera. The very term — street opera — implies impermanence; a temporary site, a modest stage quickly erected and a run of a few days. In every performing troupe, quite apart from difference in dialect, there would be difference in costuming, make-up and repertoire. This temporary stage of attap and bamboo is along Boat Quay. Rivercraft are barely visible behind.

Singapore. Commercial Square. Soldiers returning from an officiel reception Johnson Pier.

71

119 **Official Reception** c1900

Visiting royalty and other dignitaries were met with pomp and circumstance at Johnston Pier. From there they would make their way into Fullerton Square and the town. This postcard shows soldiers of the Madras Infantry Regiment marching through the square after an unspecified official reception. The Hongkong and Shanghai Bank Building is on the right.

Agri-Horticultural Show, Singapore.

THE FEDERATED ENGINEERING CO. L D. KUALA LUMPUR.

120 **Agri-Horticultural Show** 1906

The first Agri-Horticultural Show was held in Kuala Lumpur in 1904, followed by Penang in 1905 and in Singapore the following year. The show was an opportunity to see and hear of the progress made in the agricultural development of the Federated Malay States. Song Ong Siang in his book A *Hundred Years of the Chinese in Singapore* noted that more European firms than Chinese took part in the displays.

74

Decoration on King's Coronation Day, Singapore.

121 **Coronation Day** 1901

English flags, bunting and other decorations commemorate the coronation of King Edward VII in 1901 on the headquarters of Fraser and Neave. The Singapore community was represented at the coronation in London by two Queen's scholars, London educated lawyer Song Ong Siang and Cambridge educated physician Dr Lim Boon Keng. The men went as members of the Singapore Volunteer Corps.

G. P. O. Decorated During Duke of Connaught's Visit, Singapore.

122 **The Visit of the Duke of Connaught** c1905

The Duke of Connaught (brother of King Edward VII) and his wife were on their way to Japan when they stopped in Singapore for a few days in 1906. The Duchess inaugurated the clock in Victoria Memorial Hall. As with other Royal visits, the town was decorated with flags and bunting. The General Post office, shown here, was demolished in 1925 to make way for the present Fullerton building. The fountain on the right, the Tan Kim Seng Memorial Fountain was a fixture in front of the G.P.O. from 1882 until it was moved to the Esplanade when Fullerton Building was constructed.

Singapore. Royal Visit Decoration.

123 Royal Visit 1901

On April 21, 1901 the Duke and Duchess of York (later King George V and Queen Mary) arrived in Singapore for a three-day visit. It was a time of confused loyalties among the Singapore Chinese. British power and prestige was respected and western education sought, yet there was concern over preserving the roots of Chinese culture and a desire to see China reform and modernize. (Revolutionary leader Dr Sun Yat Sen visited Singapore eight times between 1900 and 1910.) The visit of the royal couple included a ricksha drive through Chinatown and the couple was presented with an album of 100 photographs from the firm of G.R. Lambert.

The Esplanade, Singapore.

124 Marching on the Esplanade c1904

Indian soldiers march under the watchful eyes of Sir Stamford Raffles. Behind is Victoria Memorial Hall under construction.

Crowds watching New Year Regatta, Singapore.

125 **New Year Regatta** c1910

The New Years sports, in which all communities participated, were considered for years to be a means of promoting racial harmony. Inevitably the boat races proved to be a day of glory for the Malays and *orang laut* (sea gypsies) who in boats of their own design would triumph over European, Chinese, Bugis and other competitors.

Decorated Street in Chinese Quarter.

126 **Decorated Street in Chinatown** c1906

The visit of the Duke of Connaught in 1906 was celebrated by the Straits Chinese British Association with spectacular arches, brilliant lanterns and illuminated dragons. A visit to Chinatown was a "must" for visiting dignitaries.

127 **Chinese Funeral** c1910

To westerners, a Chinese funeral was suitably exotic material for a fascinating postcard.

128 **Chinese Funeral** c1910

Malay Priest & his Wives

With love from dad RmS.

129 Muslim Religious Leader and Family c1920s

Singapore was an economic and cultural centre of the Malay-Muslim world in Southeast Asia by the end of the 19th century. Muslim religious publications were printed here and pilgrims came from around the region to catch the ships that would take them to Mecca. Some stayed to work and earn their passage money; others never left the island.

(26)   Malay funeral. Singapore

130 Malay Funeral c1910

This unusually tinted postcard shows a Malay funeral procession in Prinsip Street. Muslims must be buried before sunset on the actual day they die.

Road Repairing, Singapore.

131 Road Repairing c1910

Even the most mundane subjects were immortalized in postcards. The back-breaking task of road building and repair work was carried out mainly by Indians who continued to be well represented in the transport, harbour and communications workforce right up to World War II. These workers are along Beach Road. On the right is the Drill Hall, re-erected on reclaimed land from its original position at the mouth of the Singapore River around 1907.

Market Scene, Singapore

132 Market Scene c1905

"Koek's Bazaar" at Orchard Road and Cuppage Road before the construction of the brick facade. The vacant space between the market and Orchard Road had been used by vendors since 1896. The fountain on the left was removed from its original location at Telok Ayer Market around 1902. The land was originally part of the estate of William Cuppage and was bought over by his son-in-law Edwin Koek in the 1860s. Beyond this point Orchard Road became a straight, well-shaded drive leading to Tanglin. Emerald Hill before it was covered with terrace houses is visible behind.

SINGAPORE
Ship discharging coals

133 **Chinese Coolies**

The majority of early Chinese immigrants were indentured to a *kong-si* and their services were engaged through a coolie agent or headman. The *kongsi* would pay for their passage on the condition that the coolies worked for a designated length of time until all expenses incurred were duly paid off. The work they were involved in included such back-breaking tasks as loading and unloading cargo.

Singapore.

Stengel & Co., Dresden-Berlin. 12468.

Natives at work. – Eingeborene bei der Arbeit.

134 **Natives at Work** c1900

The postcards shows a rottan (rattan) factory. The skills for processing rattan were probably brought in from Guangdong, China during the 19th century. Raw rattan was imported either from China or the Dutch East Indies.

A look in the Jungle.

135 **The Jungle** c1910

A look into Singapore's lush, green jungle. The lushness of the jungle deceived early settlers into believing the island to be fertile. But early crops of nutmegs, sugar, coffee, cinammon and cloves all failed. Only the Chinese gambier and pepper plantations survived. Many of the general rural postcard scenes are difficult to locate on the island and virtually impossible to date!

Singapore. Native Village.

136 **Country Scene** c1910

This rural scene, made all the more rich by the lavish use of green tints, juxtaposes a single Malay figure with a jinricksha beside a timber kampong house along a country lane. A "classic" kampong portrait.

Singapore. Suburban, Police Station.

137 **Suburban Police Station** c1905

This postcard shows the Geylang Police station. The figures, staring rather intently out of the card, obviously posed for the photographer.

Singapore.

Country roads.

Park in Singapore

138 **Country Roads** c1900

Jinricksha and bullock cart, the two most common forms of road transport at the turn of the century, pose at the crossroads of what appears to be a coconut plantation. Coconut plantations were scattered around the area of Amber Road, Haig Road, Joo Chiat Road and Tanjong Katong around 1900.

139 **Park in Singapore** c1900

Another lush vision of tropical scenery. By the turn of the century little of Singapore's virgin jungle was left intact. A strip of vegetation in the Botanic Gardens however, was left as near to primeval jungle as possible. Other postcards with the identical photograph identify this as Orchard Road.

Singapore. Gayland Road.

140 **Geylang Road** c1905

Before World War I Geylang was a relatively quiet road. When the suburban expansion of town continued after the war, Geylang became a busy thoroughfare lined with shophouses. Along the quieter lorongs, residential terrace houses and bungalows took the place of vegetable gardens. Note the spelling 'Geyland'. The site of the Citronella Factory, which processed lemon grass for use in soaps and perfumes and closed down in the 1890s, became the eastern terminal for Singapore's first tramline.

Singapore. Scotch and Steven Rds.

141 **Scotts and Stevens Road** c1910

This picture of well shaded avenues captures a suburban scene in what is now a heavily trafficed and developed part of town.

142 **Bukit Timah Village** c1910

Although the majority of the early Chinese settled in the town some chose to settle in rural areas. This settlement grew up along Bukit Timah road near Bukit Timah (Tin Hill), the highest point on the island. Bukit Timah Road was first explored in 1827 and the road as far as Kranji was laid in the 1840s. On a clear day a fine view could be seen from the top of the hill. For many years the jungle around the hill was infested with tigers. Pits dug to entrap the animals were also a tourist attraction. The British forces made their last stand against the Japanese along Bukit Timah in February, 1942.

143 **Country Scene** c1905

The unidentified structure in the foreground appears to be a garden house or wayside resting place. Certainly it would have been an ideal resting place for nature lovers.

The Beach, Singapore

144 **The Beach** c1910

A view of the beach along the East Coast, now reclaimed, perhaps not far from the runway of today's Changi Airport.

(49)   Malay Fishing Village, Singapore.

145 **Fishing Village** 1910

Even with intensive urbanization the Malays continued to preserve much of their traditional lifestyle into the 1930s, living peacefully in kampong-style houses in the almost exclusively Malay districts of Geylang Serai, Kampong Melayu Pasir Panjang, as well as in kampongs like this along the north and east coasts of the island. For many Malays, fishing was a main source of revenue.

146 **Tanjong Katong** c1910

In the early days sugar cane and cinnamon were planted in the area but during the 1840s large tracts of land were cleared right up to Siglap for coconut plantations. Along the sea, fanciful bungalows and more modest beach structures were a cool comfortable playground for the well-to-do.

Grove Hotel and Sanatorium, Tanjong Katong   SINGAPORE

G. R. Lambert & Co., Singapore

147 **Grove Hotel** c1900

A quiet, cool retreat from city life.

Singapore. Tanjong Katong.

148 **Villa, Tanjong Katong** c1900

Many wealthy Straits-born Chinese owned such bungalows along the beach of Tanjong Katong, Tanjong Rhu and Pasir Panjang. A curious blend of European and Malay architectural features, they were designed to make full use of the pleasant sea breezes. Up to the 1950s many of the houses could still be seen along the East Coast. Some still grace Pasir Panjang, although the beach has been reclaimed.

Singapore. Tanjong Katong. Sea Side. Villa.

135

149 **Villa, Tanjong Katong** c1900

Surrounded by coconut trees and topped by a pair of cuppolas, this Straits Chinese seaside villa was also guarded by eagles at the gateposts. Horse drawn carriages wait to convey members of the family.

(47)   Pasir Panjang, Singapore.

150 **Pasir Panjang**

As business and shipping interests took over the Telok Blangah area, more Malays moved westward along the coast into Pasir Panjang.

Malay Village, Singapore.

151 **Malay Village** c1910

Singapore's intensive urbanization and increasing land values in the 1930s bore perhaps most heavily upon the Malays who wished to preserve a semi-rural way of life.

90

(42)   Malay Dwelling House, Singapore.

152 **Malay Dwelling House** c1910

In the centre of this village is a small Malay cemetery.

(9)   Malay Hawker, Singapore.

153 **Malay Hawker** c1910

Another view of kampong life. Education for the vast majority of Malay children was hampered by being tied to the British Colonial policy followed in the Malay states. This policy aimed to avoid dislocation and keep them contented in their traditional way of life by educating them to be farmers and fisherman.

154 **Natives Bathing** c1905

Chinese boys with their pigtails tied up on top of their heads take a swim in a village stream.

155 **Malay House** c1900

The house in the foreground of this classic kampong scene illustrates the traditional Malay houseplan. The *serembi* or guest verandah in front is followed by the *ibu rumah* or main body of the house. The *dapor* or kitchen is lowered and at the rear. Note the interesting timber grills and the use of boards to keep the attap roof secure.

Singapore. Malay Houses. *Nov 31 - Thursday leaving for Penang, return through the States to Port Swettenham. Arrive here about Tuesday; leave again for Java on Friday. C.*

Malay Kampong c1900

Another rural scene.

Singapore. Malay Houses.

157 **Malay Houses** c1900

Orang laut of Pulau Brani pose in front of their houses on stilts.

93

INDEX

Numbers refer to the postcard illustrations, except those preceded by 'p' which refer to page numbers.

Bras Basah Road, Singapore.

Hill Street, Singapore

(4) Boat Quay, Singapore.

Times Editions would like to extend special thanks to
Andrew Tan Kim Guan and Koh Seow Chuan for the
use of the postcards from their private collections.

First printed in conjunction with the
National Archives Postcard Exhibition, August, 1986

Publisher's Number: 306